PONTIAC'S WAR

On May 9, 1763, an Ottawa Indian named Pontiac directed an attack by his warriors against the British fort at Detroit. His aim was to punish the British for the injustices he felt they had done his people and to reinstate the French, who had formerly controlled the Great Lakes area. The war quickly spread from Detroit until it engulfed almost the entire Indian world. Its effects were to change forever the relations between the Indian and the English-speaking white man, between England and her North American colonies, and between the people on the frontier and the inhabitants of the farms and towns of the thirteen colonies.

PRINCIPALS

GENERAL SIR JEFFREY AMHERST — Commander-in-chief of British armed forces in North America.

HENRY BOUQUET — Colonel in the British army; commander at the Battle of Bushy Run.

GEORGE CROGHAN — Indian agent for the Crown, and trader.

JAMES DALYELL — Captain in the British army and aide-de-camp to General Amherst; commander at the Battle of Bloody Bridge.

HENRY GLADWIN — Major in the British army; commander at Fort Detroit.

SIR WILLIAM JOHNSON — Superintendent of Indian Affairs.

PONTIAC — War chief of the Ottawa nation encamped at Detroit.

ROBERT ROGERS — Major in the British army; commander during the French and Indian War of Rogers' Rangers.

"The Black Watch at Bushy Run," a watercolor by C. W. Jefferys. (Courtesy Imperial Oil Collection)

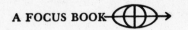

Pontiac's War, 1763-1766

The Indians' Greatest Uprising Fails to Stop Westward Expansion

by David Goodnough

FRANKLIN WATTS, INC.

575 Lexington Avenue   New York, N.Y. 10022

The authors and publisher of the Focus Books wish to acknowledge the helpful editorial suggestions of Professor Richard B. Morris.

Cover photograph, "Pontiac in Council," courtesy New York Public Library, Picture Collection.

FOR DORIS

SBN 531-01018-X
Library of Congress Catalog Card Number: 77-119576
Printed in the United States of America

Contents

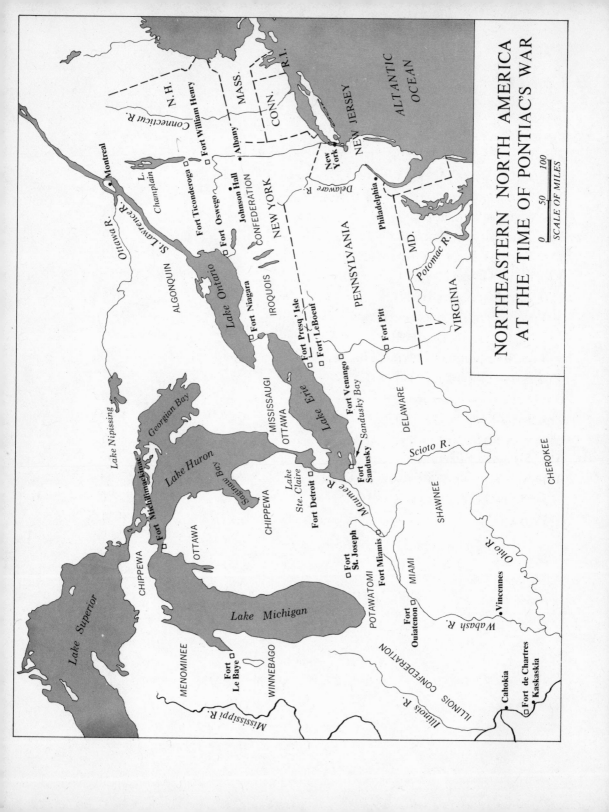

NORTHEASTERN NORTH AMERICA
AT THE TIME OF PONTIAC'S WAR

SCALE OF MILES
0   50   100

Introduction

The French and Indian War, the fourth conflict between France and England to take place on the North American continent, ended in September of 1760. At Montreal the governor of Canada, the Marquis de Vaudreuil, surrendered his army to Sir Jeffrey Amherst, the commander-in-chief of British forces. Thus ended a struggle that had extended over almost three-quarters of a century. England now possessed, as a prize of war, all of the land from the Atlantic coast of the thirteen British colonies and Canada to the Mississippi River. This was a vast wilderness which could be crossed only by following the water routes composed of lakes and rivers and the portages (short overland routes) connecting them. Much of this land had never been seen by Englishmen, and General Amherst was anxious to have the French forts of the far west occupied by British troops as soon as possible. He wanted to make British possession of the forts a fact before the diplomats met to work out a formal treaty.

On the very next day after the surrender of Canada, Amherst directed the American colonial officer Major Robert Rogers to proceed to the west with two companies of his famous Rogers' Rangers. His mission was to occupy the string of forts that France had built to safeguard the route from Canada to her province in Louisiana in the south. These forts were built at the most crucial portages in the northeastern part of the North American continent. They not only protected and offered shelter to traders but also allowed their garrisons to watch over the Indian population of the land. Indians usually gathered near the settlements of the white men in order to trade with them or purchase services which only white men could perform, such as the repair of firearms.

Major Robert Rogers, commander of the famed Rogers' Rangers. (National Archives)

Robert Rogers' Mission

Rogers' mission was a dangerous one, for no British soldiers, except captives, had ever been in any of the French forts. No one knew the temper of the French garrisons or of the Indians who were friendly to the French.

Rogers left Montreal on September 13, 1760, with 200 men in 15 whaleboats, and set out for the western forts. The first of these was Fort Niagara, which controlled the most strategic portage on the continent —

the passage from Lake Ontario that ran up the Niagara River, past Niagara Falls, and thence to Lake Erie. Niagara had been captured from the French in 1759 and was already occupied by British troops. After leaving Niagara, Rogers camped at Presqu'Isle (present-day Erie, Pennsylvania) on the shore of Lake Erie to await a detachment of British soldiers from Fort Pitt, 100 miles to the south, who were to garrison the fort at Detroit. Indian messengers were sent ahead to inform the Indians and French at Detroit that Rogers was on his way to accept their surrender.

On November 29, 1760, Major Rogers accepted the French surrender at Detroit in a colorful ceremony in which the green-clad Rangers, the red-coated British, the white-coated French, and over 700 Indians, in all their finery, participated. The French flag was lowered and the oath of allegiance to England was administered to all of the French *habitants*, members of the agricultural community the French had established to supply the fort. The French garrison was sent back to Fort Pitt as prisoners to be exchanged for British prisoners still held by the French.

Rogers next sent a detachment of Rangers to accept the surrender of — and to occupy — Fort Miamis between the Maumee and Wabash rivers and Fort Ouiatenon on the Wabash River. Rogers had hoped to secure Fort Michilimackinac, the extremely strategic strong point at the juncture of Lake Michigan and Lake Huron, but was prevented by the severe winter weather.

The following summer, 1761, a grand council with the Indians was held at Detroit, with Sir William Johnson, superintendent of Indian affairs, attending. The purpose of the council was to assure the western Indians that the British planned no radical changes in the system of trading that had been set up by the French. It also sought to quell rumors that had been spread by some Indians and French that the British intended to cut off their supply of gunpowder, which the French had always supplied freely.

Major Henry Gladwin was ordered by General Amherst to take command of the western territory, to occupy the remaining French forts, and to keep the peace until a formal treaty was completed with France. Gladwin was thirty-two years old and had served in America since 1755, both as a field officer (he was wounded during the French and Indian War) and as commander of a wilderness fort. He was an unspectacular soldier, but his reliability and steadiness had earned him Amherst's deepest respect. Furthermore, his long service in the wilderness had taught him respect for the Indians' fighting ability, a feeling which was rare in British officers of that day.

Gladwin arrived at Detroit in September, but was too ill to take part in the council or to proceed with his mission. He sent Captain Henry Balfour north with 120 men to occupy Fort Michilimackinac, which had been abandoned by the French. There Balfour left 28 men, under the command of Lieutenant William Leslye, and proceeded to the fort at La Baye (present-day Green Bay, Wisconsin), which had also been abandoned. This fort controlled the route from Lake Michigan to the Wisconsin River and the Upper Mississippi River and drew the trade of the far western Indians.

Captain Balfour renamed the fort Edward Augustus and left Ensign James Gorrell in command of 17 men. Balfour next returned to Lake Michigan and rowed south to the fort on the St. Joseph River on the Michigan side of the lake. This fort controlled the passage from Lake Michigan to the French settlements on the Middle Mississippi River. Fifteen men were left as garrison, under the command of Ensign Francis Schlosser. Balfour, having completed the circle of the northern posts, returned to Detroit with the 15 men he had left.

Meanwhile, the members of Rogers' Rangers who had been left as garrison at Fort Miamis and Fort Ouiatenon had been relieved. Ensign Robert Holmes was put in command of Miamis with 15 men, and Lieutenant Edward Jenkins with 20 men at Fort Ouiatenon.

A new blockhouse was constructed at the old British trading post at Sandusky on the south shore of Lake Erie. It was built by Lieutenant Elias Meyer, who was also its commander with a garrison of 15 men. He was later relieved by Ensign Christopher Pauli. The building of this blockhouse disturbed the Indians, since it was their understanding that the British were merely to occupy the French forts and not build new ones. To the Indians, the forts were a convenience; they had permitted the French to build them because they made trade easier. To the British, the forts were strong points from which they could control a subjected people, and they could and should be built wherever necessary.

Although Fort de Chartres on the Mississippi River and Vincennes on the Wabash River were still in the hands of the French, the Great Lakes area now seemed firmly under the control of the British. However, the number of British soldiers west of Niagara and Fort Pitt was no more than 250. These men were given the task of ordering the commerce and the very lives of far larger numbers of colonials and natives. Their tools were discipline, organization, and perseverance — qualities that were usually lacking in their charges. But at this early stage, they were to meet one Indian who seemed to possess all of these.

The Plot Against Detroit

On the morning of May 7, 1763, Major Henry Gladwin, of the 80th Regiment of Light Armed Foot and commander of the garrison at Fort Detroit, stepped out of the council house inside the fort and prepared to meet a delegation of Indians. The Indians were led by Pontiac, a chief of the Ottawa nation, whom Gladwin had first met the previous week. It was the custom for the Indians of the Great Lakes to return to the forts in the spring to trade the furs they had gathered during the winter. Here they also prepared for their summer activities, the most important of which was usually warfare with their traditional enemies in the south. Pontiac had requested that he and his braves be permitted to enter the fort to dance the calumet (peace pipe) dance. Gladwin had allowed him and forty of his followers to enter the fort, where they leaped about and shouted and sang of their deeds in war. Although Gladwin was not aware of it then, several of the Indians detached themselves from the celebration and wandered freely through the fort, inspecting the layout and defenses. Pontiac then left, promising to return in a few days for a more elaborate ceremony which would include many of his nation who had not yet returned from their winter hunting.

Sometime between Pontiac's leaving and his next appearance, Gladwin had learned that the Indians were plotting to attack the fort. Their plan was to enter the fort in order to dance the calumet and ensure the British commanders of their wish to live in peace and harmony with their new white neighbors. But under the blankets they wore wrapped around them they would carry rifles whose barrels had been sawed off to make them easier to conceal. At a signal from Pontiac, the Indians were to throw off their robes, fire into the British guard, then open the gates to the hundreds of warriors waiting outside.

However, Gladwin was forewarned and prepared. Every soldier in the fort was armed and at his post; and the British civilians, the traders and trappers who did business with the Indians, were on the alert within the houses that bordered on the square. The Indians walked into an armed camp.

Pontiac was about fifty years old, a tall man of six feet or over. He addressed the younger Gladwin angrily: "We are greatly surprised, brother, at this unusual step thou hast taken, to have all the soldiers under arms, and that thy young chiefs are not at council as formerly. We would be very glad to know the reason for this, for we imagine some bad bird has given thee ill news of us, which we advise thee not to believe, my brother, for there are bad birds who want to stir thee up against thy brothers, the Indians, who have been always in perfect friendship with their brothers, the English."

Gladwin replied that he expected delegations from some of the other Indian nations who were coming in from their winter hunting. He wanted

Council between Pontiac and Gladwin. Pontiac is shown holding a belt of wampum, a device used to aid the memory of the speaker. Symbols containing the main points of a speech were woven into the belt. (New York Public Library)

to have the garrison under arms when they arrived, since he did not trust them as he did his friends the Ottawas, who would not be offended by such measures. This was obviously a lie, and Pontiac knew it, but he could do nothing. He continued with his speech, in which he told Gladwin of the death of six of the Ottawas' chiefs and hoped that Gladwin would give them some presents to ease their sorrow. It was sometime during this speech that Pontiac was to give the signal for the Indians to start the hoped-for massacre. Whatever the signal was supposed to be, it was never given. Gladwin presented Pontiac with some clothing and bread and tobacco in memory of the dead chiefs. The council was ended, and the Indians returned to their village, furious with the British and with Pontiac for not giving the signal. Many said they would gladly have risked death at the hands of the guard in order to get at the British "dogs."

Pontiac assured his people that he intended to make war upon the British, but he still hoped to take them by surprise. The next day, Sunday, May 8, he and three other chiefs had a meeting with Gladwin in which Pontiac assured him of the devotion of the Indians to the British, which he proved by placing a calumet in Gladwin's hands. He then said that he would bring his young warriors to the fort on the next day so that they might all smoke the peace pipe and banish any suspicion from the minds of the British. Gladwin was not taken in by the speech. He said that he would admit the chiefs, but could see no reason for allowing young warriors in the fort. After Pontiac left, Gladwin increased the guard and set his men to strengthening the defenses of the fort. He also offered shelter to those families, particularly the British families, living outside the fort.

Shortly before noon of the next day, Monday, May 9, Pontiac and his Ottawa warriors approached the fort. Gladwin sent his interpreters to inform them that only the chiefs would be allowed to enter. Pontiac replied that if all of his people were not allowed to smell the smoke of the peace pipe, they would throw away the belt of friendship they had received from Sir William Johnson two years previously. Gladwin said that he would allow small parties in one at a time to enjoy the festivities.

This enraged Pontiac, and finally convinced that his strategy had failed, he ordered his people to return to their village. There he snatched up a tomahawk and began chanting his fierce song of war. If he could not attack the British dogs in their fort then he would kill all he could find outside, and would cut off the fort and force it to surrender. His warriors were now in a frenzy, and ready to undertake any violence, even though

[14]

attacking an armed fort was against all their traditions of warfare. Pontiac ordered his village relocated in a more strategic position, closer to the fort. He then divided his warriors into small war parties and sent them against the British civilians who had not sought the safety of the fort.

One party attacked the farmhouse of a Mrs. Turnbull, who lived alone with her two sons across the river from the fort. The Indians burst upon them with no warning and killed all three. The scalping cries that accompanied the deed were heard within the fort. They were, in effect, a declaration of war.

Another party crossed over by canoe to Isle au Cochon (present-day Belle Isle) to seize the cattle grazing there. There were eleven people on the island: two soldiers who were acting as herdsmen for the cows; a retired soldier named Fisher who lived on a farm with his wife, four children, and a serving woman; a French workman who was making some repairs on the Fishers' house; and another soldier who was visiting from the fort. The Ottawas again struck without warning and killed two of the soldiers, Fisher, his wife and one child. The French worker tried to escape and was also killed when the warriors mistook him for an Englishman. The rest of the people on the island were taken prisoner.

These nine deaths were the first of more than two thousand which were to take place in the next three years. The actions in which they occurred, together with an unparalleled series of military disasters suffered by the British, have been called at different times "The Conspiracy of Pontiac," "Pontiac's Revolt," and "Pontiac's War." Whatever it was, it was to change forever the relations between the Indian and the English-speaking white man, between England and her North American colonies, and between the people on the frontier and the inhabitants of the farms and towns of the thirteen colonies. And at its heart stood one man.

Pontiac and the Ottawa Nation

Little is known of Pontiac before the war that was to bear his name, except that he was a war chief of the Ottawas. Like most Indian nations, the Ottawas had two classes of chiefs — civil chiefs and war chiefs. The civil chiefs were usually older men who had earned the respect of their people through their wisdom, eloquence, and abilities. War chiefs attained their position through their courage, their fighting ability, and above all their success in war. Indian warriors looked to their more successful members —those who had taken more scalps or prisoners — for leadership, and they would follow them as long as they continued in their winning ways. But once a war chief met defeat, or a series of reversals, or just plain bad luck, his followers would desert him for any other war chief they favored. As impermanent as their leadership was, war chiefs nevertheless had more influence in tribal affairs than the civil chiefs, and many times led their followers to take a course of action condemned by the older chiefs.

The Ottawa nation was once part of a single Indian nation that had emigrated to the Great Lakes from the northeastern Atlantic seaboard. In time this one nation split into three — the Ottawas, the Chippewas, and the Potawatomies. At the end of the French and Indian War, the Ottawas had a large village near the fort at Detroit and smaller villages at Saginaw Bay and Michilimackinac. The Potawatomies also had a village at Detroit and another across the Michigan peninsula at the St. Joseph River. The Chippewas gathered mostly at Saginaw Bay, Michilimackinac, and on the peninsula that divides Lake Superior and Lake Michigan. Of these three nations, the Ottawas were the least influenced by the French missionaries who circulated among them. Christianity, which was perhaps the only humanizing influence the white man had on the Indian, failed to impress them. As a result, they gained eminence as the most savage of the Great

Lakes tribes. They were the most eager to make war, and the most brutal in their pursuit of it.

During the French and Indian War, the French made good use of the Indians camped around Detroit. War parties were sent to aid in the defense of Fort Duquesne at the forks of the Ohio River. Indians participated in the disastrous defeat of Major General Edward Braddock who had led an expedition of 2,500 men from Virginia to expel the French "invaders" who had built their fort on land claimed by England.

Ottawas had also been in the army of Marquis de Montcalm when he left Montreal and invaded New York by way of Lake Champlain in 1757. This campaign culminated in the massacre at Fort William Henry on Lake George. About fifty English men and women were killed and over two hundred taken captive when the Indians in Montcalm's army attacked the British after the fort had surrendered and the defenders had laid down their arms.

The next year, 1758, found the Detroit Indians once again at the forks of the Ohio. They had rallied there to defend Fort Duquesne against another British attempt to seize the fort. The large British force advancing on the fort was under the command of Brigadier General John Forbes. An advance force which was cutting a new road through the wilderness was under the command of a Swiss mercenary, Colonel Henry Bouquet. The building of the road went slowly, and both sides grew impatient to attack. The British were the first to move. Major James Grant had persuaded Bouquet, who was normally the most cautious of soldiers, to allow him to dash to Fort Duquesne and surprise the enemy. Grant and his army of 842, who were mostly Scottish Highlanders, managed to reach the vicinity of the fort undetected, but Grant promptly threw away any chance of surprise by ordering his bagpipers to play while his men marched in closed ranks toward the fort. The Indians, thus forewarned, lay in ambush and were soon rewarded. Two hundred and seventy British troops were killed, 42 were wounded, and 100 taken prisoner.

Grant's defeat took place in September, late in the year for the Indians, who were eager to return to their villages to prepare for their winter hunting. Quite satisfied with their victory, they considered their services to the French fulfilled, and abandoned them to the advancing main army of the British and returned to Detroit. In November, the French burned their fort and fled to Fort Venango, on the Allegheny River. The British occupied the abandoned fort and immediately began to rebuild it. They named it Fort Pitt.

In 1759, a large British army, accompanied by 900 Iroquois warriors under Sir William Johnson, had laid siege to the French fort at Niagara early in July. The French had gathered a sizable force of Indians to attack Fort Pitt, but they rushed north when they heard of the attack on Niagara. The British, now under the command of Johnson (their original commander had been killed in the siege), learned of this relief column and prepared an ambush about three miles up the portage road from the fort. For once, the French and their Indians were on the receiving end of an ambush, and they were spared none of the horror. The fierce Seneca Indians, the most war-loving of the Iroquois, attacked the column's flank with such fury that the whole force broke and ran. The Iroquois pursued them for five miles. The French and Indian losses were reported to be 500 killed and 120 captured, a crushing blow to the French forces of the west. The garrison at Fort Niagara, all hope of reinforcement gone, surrendered.

The fall of Niagara convinced the Indians that it was time to make peace overtures to the British. They knew that it would be useless to make any last-ditch defense against an army that, despite some previous crushing defeats, was still conquering one French stronghold after another. Their decision to abandon the French was in keeping with their customs. The French commanders were, in effect, war chiefs: they organized and directed war parties. And war chiefs could command the allegiance of their warriors only as long as they were successful. The French commanders were no longer successful.

"The most strategic point in North America." Fort Niagara at the mouth of the Niagara River. This view is to the south. The highway on the left bank of the Niagara River follows the old portage road. (Courtesy Power Authority of the State of New York)

Added to this, of course, was the Indians' knowledge that whichever side won, they would still have to deal with the white man for the absolutely essential trade goods such as powder and shot. The British sent delegations to the Indians to assure them that once the French were driven from the land, everything would return to normal, with no disruption in trade. Indeed, the situation would be better, for British trade goods were far superior to French. They also gave the Indians generous gifts, as a sample of what would be in store for them if they were friendly to the British.

After the fall of Fort Niagara, the Detroit Indians returned to their villages to await the next move of the British. The French enlarged and strengthened their fort in expectation of the attack they were sure would come. The British, however, struck to the east, at Quebec and Montreal, and obtained their prize without having to strike farther west.

The end of the war found the Ottawa Indians deeply divided between those who favored coming to terms with the British and those who remained loyal to the French. So deep was this division that many of the Ottawas left Detroit and settled at the mouth of the Cuyahoga River (present-day Cleveland) on the southern shore of Lake Erie. Prominent among the Ottawas who remained at Detroit was Chief Pontiac.

The Causes of Pontiac's War

The surrender of Canada to the English did not end the war between England and France. Rather, it was just one victory, although a tremendous one, in a worldwide struggle which in Europe was called the Seven Years' War. The French, although they had lost Canada, still held their province of Louisiana and the forts on the Mississippi River and at Vincennes on the Wabash — and the majority of the white men who lived near the western forts were French. Many of these Frenchmen never recognized the French defeat, and continued to encourage the Indians to make trouble for the English. They spread rumors among the western tribes that the English intended to destroy them by cutting off their supply of the precious gunpowder and shot which they needed for their hunting.

Despite the promises made to the Indians at Detroit by Sir William Johnson in 1761, the official English policy, as set by General Amherst, was to deny them the use of gunpowder and to cease the flow of gifts by which the traders and administrators had kept them satisfied. When they returned from their winter hunting in the spring of 1762, the Indians found no gifts waiting for them as was the custom with the French, and there was little or no ammunition to replenish their stock. Added to this were the English ban on rum and irregularities in the prices offered for the furs the Indians brought in for exchange for trade goods. Luckily, there were many new traders at the forts now that hostilities had technically ceased, and the Indians managed to obtain enough powder on credit to see them through the summer.

Practically every white man with any knowledge of Indians thought Amherst's policy of stringency was foolhardy. Captain Donald Campbell, who had commanded at Detroit until Gladwin's arrival, wrote privately to Colonel Bouquet: "The general [Amherst] says the Crown is to be no longer at the expense of maintaining the Indians, that they may very well live by their hunting, and desires to keep them scarce of powder. I should be glad to know what you do in that respect. I am certain if the Indians in this country had the least hint that we intended to prevent them from the use of ammunition, it would be impossible to keep them down."

General Amherst, who was looking forward to his return to England and an honorable retirement, did not listen to any of them. He considered the Indians little more than beggars. True, they were useful in war, but now that it was settled, let them shift for themselves. Like many another administrator in the face of a peoples' helplessness against forces they could not control, he preached self-reliance.

Dissatisfaction with the policy of the English soon became almost universal among the Indians, but they could do little about it, since they were entirely dependent upon the white man for ammunition and the repair of firearms. This dissatisfaction found expression in the preachings of a Delaware Indian who lived in the Ohio River valley. The "Delaware Prophet," as he was called, claimed to be divinely inspired, and Indians traveled from far and wide to hear him. His stern message was that the Indian nations had fallen into sin by adopting the ways of the white man, and that their only hope of salvation was to purify themselves by throwing away the arms of the white man and returning to their original state. This meant building their own fires without the use of flint, making their own clothing, and, above all, hunting with bow and arrow. The Delaware Prophet had a strong influence on all the Indians who heard him, and they spread his teachings from village to village until they were known to all. For once, all of the nations agreed: White men — or, at least, the British — were an evil influence and must be driven from the land. The time was ripe for revolt; all that was lacking was a leader.

The Indian world was now whipped into turmoil. In the east, the Iroquois, who had faithfully supported the English in the war, discovered that they had also helped open the frontier to settlement by the white man. Settlers were pouring over the mountains, using the trails the army had opened up. The Senecas, the most numerous and troublesome to the white man of all the Iroquois, were so dissatisfied that they conceived of a general uprising of all Indians against the British. They even went so far as to send war belts (pieces of wampum containing symbols which expressed, in a sort of shorthand, the speech which the bearer delivered) to the other tribes. Farther west and in the south, the French were still in control of the forts on the Wabash, the Illinois, and the Mississippi, and did not feel that they were bound by the terms of the surrender of Canada. They continued to carry on the war by stirring up the Indians against the British and assuring them of aid should they revolt.

But it was the Indians at Detroit who were at the center of the entire Indian world, and they felt the mounting pressures from the Senecas in the east and from the French in the west and south. Pontiac, who was an accomplished orator, naturally took an important part in all of the councils that were called to consider what action should be taken. In his speeches he preached his version of the utterances of the Delaware Prophet — chiefly that the British must be driven from the land. Pontiac successfully incited the Indians of the three villages around Detroit to attack the fort. Messages were sent to nearby tribes to join them if they

Pontiac in council. (New York Public Library)

pleased, but there apparently was no thought of a general uprising. Pontiac's objective was the capture of Detroit and the punishment and expulsion of the English in his immediate area. If he had a larger plan in mind, there was no evidence of it in his speeches which were recorded by white men, mostly French, who attended the councils leading up to the attack on Detroit.

The Siege of Detroit

After Pontiac's warriors returned from their attacks on the British outside the fort, they turned to the fort itself. A group of Ottawas got to

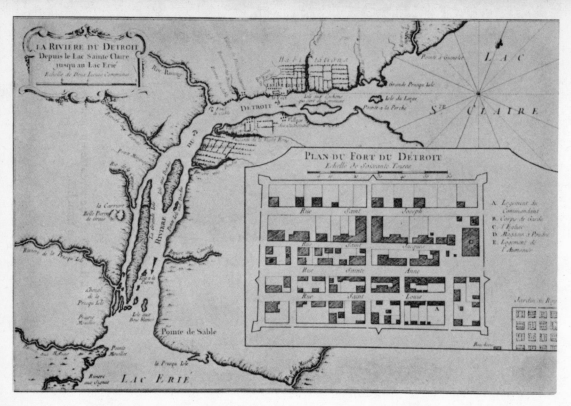

A contemporary map of the Detroit River, with an inset showing the plan of the fort. (Library of Congress)

within one hundred feet of the walls and opened fire on the garrison and on the schooner *Huron*, which was anchored in the Detroit River. Their fire was returned, but with little effect.

Fort Detroit was built on a slope leading down to the river, which meant that anyone standing on the opposite bank could look directly into the fort. It was surrounded by a high stockade, which was fairly strong but made of wood. Indian fire arrows could destroy all or part of it, as well as the wooden houses within the fort. The British reduced the threat to the stockade by banking earth against it on the inside, but there was no way to fireproof the houses. A constant fire watch was necessary, with supplies of water always ready. Although the fact that the fort was built

[24]

on a slope was a disadvantage, it had been built there for one reason: ready access to the water. The fort had a water gate which allowed vessels to load and unload men and material in relative safety. At the time of the attack, Gladwin had two ships, the two-masted schooner *Huron* and the large sloop *Michigan*. He anchored them to the north and south of the fort and used their firepower as part of his defense.

The garrison at Detroit consisted of two companies of Royal Americans (colonial troops) and a company of Queen's Rangers, plus the ships' crews — probably no more than 125 men. There were also about 20 English traders who could be called on for help during an all-out assault. Against them Pontiac had assembled 800 or 900 warriors.

Before Pontiac's plot had been discovered, a party of twelve men under Lieutenant Charles Robertson had gone north by boat across Lake Ste. Claire to take depth soundings. On May 7 a group of Chippewas from Saginaw Bay, who had been told by Pontiac of the party's whereabouts, ambushed them, killing Robertson and three others and taking the rest prisoner.

That evening Pontiac called a meeting of Indian leaders and French *habitants*, who were generally in favor of Pontiac's plans, to discuss strategy. They decided to call for an armistice while delegations from the two sides talked peace. Pontiac informed Gladwin of this decision and he agreed to the armistice. Pontiac sent four chiefs to the fort to request that Captain Campbell, who had commanded the fort before Gladwin's arrival and knew Pontiac well, be sent to the Indian camp to negotiate. Gladwin was reluctant to let Campbell go, but the captain was sure that he could talk reason to Pontiac, and besides, the respect of Indians for ambassadors was well known. Campbell, with Lieutenant George McDougall, who had volunteered to accompany him, was taken to the home of Antoine Cuillerier, a prominent *habitant* whom Pontiac intended to put in command of the fort if it capitulated. There Pontiac told them that they could have peace only if they abandoned their arms and the fort and marched under an Indian escort to the frontier. Furthermore, Campbell and Mc-

Dougall would have to remain in Pontiac's camp until the terms were accepted. Thus Pontiac violated one of the most basic of Indian traditions — the safety of ambassadors. Gladwin replied that he would not continue with negotiations until his two officers were returned to him. The siege continued.

During the short armistice, Gladwin had bought all of the surplus supplies from the *habitants* and had them moved into the fort. Pontiac subsequently informed all of the *habitants* that they must supply his warriors with food and powder or suffer the consequences of an Indian raid to acquire them. He also threatened a band of Christianized Hurons, who lived across the Detroit River and had not taken part in any of the fighting thus far, that if they did not join him he would destroy them. The Hurons had no choice but to join Pontiac, and promptly proved to be among the most effective of his warriors. On Friday, after Mass, they crossed the river and joining a group of Potawatomies, began to fire at the fort. A group of Indians occupied some houses one hundred yards from the fort, but were sent flying when Gladwin fired some hot shots at them, setting the houses afire. In the exchange the Indians lost three or four men, and they proposed a truce while they buried their dead. Gladwin used the truce to send out parties to destroy the rest of the houses within range of the fort. He feared an all-out attack, but was assured by more experienced Indian fighters that Pontiac would never risk losing the number of men necessary to take the fort in a charge.

The Fall of the Forts

The war was now a week old, and Pontiac was in no better position than he had been at the start. Furthermore, he had broken his word by imprisoning Campbell and McDougall, and had revealed to his followers that he really did not know how to take the fort. If he did not have a victory soon, his status as a war chief would be in danger. Accordingly he sent out two parties to seek allies in the vicinity of Sandusky and St. Joseph and to attack the forts there, using the same tactics that had failed at Detroit. They were not to fail again.

On May 16 the party that had been sent to Sandusky approached the fort there in the company of the Huron Indians who lived around the fort. They asked the commander, Ensign Christopher Pauli, if they could come into the fort for a council. Pauli, who had no way of knowing what had happened at Detroit, admitted seven of his formerly friendly neighbors. Shortly after they had all seated themselves for council, two Indians on either side of Pauli seized him and carried him from the cabin. Pauli was horrified to see that every one of the fifteen men in his command had been slaughtered. The traders who did their business in the fort were also killed and their supplies captured. The attack had been sudden, noiseless, and complete — with no casualties to the Indians.

Pauli was taken to Detroit, where the victorious Indians were greeted with wild joy. Pauli was made to run the gauntlet — a corridor formed by two rows of warriors who struck him with sticks, stones, clubs, and anything else they could lay their hands on. Next to torture by fire, it was the worst of the ordeals that Indians reserved for prisoners. Pauli somehow made it through the gauntlet, and was promptly adopted by a squaw to take the place of her dead husband. This was an ancient Indian custom, and the squaw's choice had to be respected. Ensign Pauli was thus spared further punishment.

On May 21, Gladwin sent the sloop *Michigan*, under the command of a Captain Newman, to the mouth of the Detroit River to await and protect some British supply boats that were due to arrive. Pontiac led two attacks on the sloop, but the Indians were easily fended off by the ship's crew and the soldiers aboard. However, the sloop's persistence in maintaining its position at the mouth of the river made it clear to Pontiac that the British were expecting either supplies or reinforcements by this route. He sent a party of Indians to move eastward along the northern shore of Lake Erie to attack any British force sent from Niagara. They were to be rewarded sooner than they expected.

Lieutenant Abraham Cuyler of the Queen's Rangers had no reason to expect any trouble from Indians. He had left Fort Niagara on May 13 in command of 96 men and with 139 barrels of supplies for the garrison at Detroit. They traveled in ten bateaux — sturdy flat-bottomed boats that were the mainstay of wilderness supply. On the night of May 28 they landed and beached their bateaux at Point Pelee, about 25 miles east of the Detroit River, and prepared to set up camp. Suddenly, a man who had been sent out to fetch firewood burst into camp with the terrifying news that they were surrounded by Indians. Lieutenant Cuyler quickly arranged his men in a semicircle with their backs to the boats. The first rush of the Indians, however, broke through the ring and threw the soldiers into confusion. The men broke and ran for the boats. Only two boats managed to escape. Lieutenant Cuyler, though wounded, made it to one of them. He had only 40 men left and little ammunition or supplies. He decided to return to Niagara.

The Indians ordered their prisoners to proceed with the eight remaining bateaux to the Detroit River. Captain Newman, who feared another attack and had grown weary of waiting for the reinforcements, had sailed for Niagara, so the victorious Indians had free passage of the river. As dawn broke on May 30, the garrison at Detroit was cheered by the sight of their expected reinforcements moving slowly up the river. But their joy turned to dismay when they saw that each boat contained Indian guards over the boatmen. As the boats passed the fort, the Indians began hooting at and insulting the soldiers who lined the stockade. Four soldiers in the lead boat took this opportunity to throw their Indian captors overboard and row furiously for the anchored schooner. The Indians managed to pull one of the men overboard and drown him, but the others were able to reach the protection of the schooner, taking with them seven barrels of supplies.

The victory at Sandusky and the capture of most of Cuyler's detachment put the Indians in a joyous mood. Unfortunately, the supplies taken from Cuyler contained a generous store of rum. In the drunken spree that followed, and which lasted for three days, all of the prisoners were killed.

The victories away from Detroit apparently inspired Pontiac to broaden the theater of the war. If he could not take Detroit, there were plenty of other forts to be taken. Furthermore, victories at the other forts would serve to enlist the nearby Indian nations in his cause. Pontiac's attack on Detroit began to take on the dimensions of a general Indian uprising.

The first fort to fall under this new plan was Fort St. Joseph, across the Michigan peninsula from Detroit. The tactics used by the Indians were the same as those they used at Sandusky. A party of Indians who had just arrived from Detroit wished to greet the fort's commander, Ensign Francis Schlosser. Once inside the fort, the Indians seized Schlosser and killed all but six of Schlosser's fifteen-man garrison. Schlosser was taken to Detroit where he was later exchanged for Indian prisoners held by the British.

The next fort to fall was Miamis (present-day Fort Wayne, Indiana) at the Maumee-Wabash portage. Here, however, the British were prepared. Ensign Robert Holmes, the fort's commander, had heard that there was some Indian trouble to the north and had put the fort off-limits to all Indians. Pontiac's warriors learned from the Miamis that they would not be allowed in the fort, so they improvised a new tactic. It was well known that Ensign Holmes kept an Indian girl as his mistress, and the girl made no secret of the fact that she hated Holmes. Pontiac's warriors sent the girl to the fort to tell Holmes that a squaw was lying ill in a nearby cabin and wished Holmes to come and treat her. Holmes agreed to come and followed the girl outside the fort, where he was promptly shot to death. Holmes's next in command, a sergeant, rushed out of the fort when he heard the shots and was seized by the Indians. The eleven soldiers left in the fort quickly shut the gates and manned the stockade. The Indians sent a British prisoner to demand that they surrender or be destroyed. The soldiers, without an officer or a sergeant, decided to surrender. The Indians took four of them back to Detroit to show before Pontiac. What happened to the other seven is not known.

Pontiac's warriors proceeded down the Wabash River to Fort Ouiatenon (present-day Lafayette, Indiana), where Lieutenant Edward Jenkins commanded a garrison of twenty men. Here they repeated their ruse of requesting a council with the commander. Jenkins left the fort to meet them and was quickly captured. The Indians demanded that Jenkins order his men to lay down their arms and surrender the fort or be killed, and Jenkins quickly capitulated. The Indians kept their word, perhaps because Fort Ouiatenon was close to French territory, and the French might not look kindly on a massacre occurring in the neighborhood of their own forts. Jenkins and his men were spared. They were taken to Fort de Chartres on the Mississippi and released.

The Fall of Fort Michilimackinac

Fort Michilimackinac was the largest English post west of Detroit. It had a garrison of thirty-five men, now commanded by Captain George Etherington with two other officers, Lieutenant William Leslye and Lieutenant John Jamet. The fall of Michilimackinac is a classic of Indian ingenuity.

On June 2 a group of Chippewas started to play a game of lacrosse with some visiting Sauk Indians just outside the fort. Lacrosse was taken

The infamous game of lacrosse at Fort Michilimackinac. (National Archives)

very seriously by Indians and was usually a part of the festivities whenever two tribes or nations got together. Since it was the king of England's birthday, a holiday air prevailed. The gates of the fort were left open and many of the soldiers strolled out to watch the game. Several squaws wandered idly into the fort. One of the players looped the ball high over the stockade wall and both teams ran past the amused soldiers and through the gate in pursuit of the ball. Inside the fort they threw away their sticks and caught up the weapons that the squaws had concealed under their robes. They then began to attack the surprised soldiers and English traders. The French inhabitants of the fort locked themselves in their houses and were not touched. Captain Etherington and Lieutenant Leslye were quickly captured, but Lieutenant Jamet fought furiously with his sword until he was finally wounded. An Indian leaped upon him and cut off his head. Twenty soldiers and one trader were killed in a matter of minutes.

The attack at Michilimackinac had not been undertaken at the urging of Pontiac's warriors, but had been planned and executed by a Chippewa war chief named Matchekewis. He had heard of Pontiac's successes to the south and decided to act before another nation received the glory of capturing the fort. His action, however, infuriated the northern branch of the Ottawa nation, which lived near L'Arbre Croche (present-day Cross Village, Michigan), twenty miles to the south. They had received a war belt from Pontiac urging them to join in the uprising, but had not yet decided what to do. Now that Michilimackinac had fallen, they felt cheated of the only prize they stood to gain in the war. Furthermore, Matchekewis had not informed them of his intention to attack the fort. Indian diplomacy demanded that any war chief who decided to take up the hatchet must inform his neighbors and invite them along. The enraged Ottawas hurried to the fort and forced the Chippewas to turn over all the British prisoners to them. The Chippewas, of course, objected, and a two-day council was held to settle the differences. The Ottawas were given part of the captured stores and eleven soldiers, Captain Etherington, Lieutenant Leslye, and two traders. The Chippewas received the greater part of the captured supplies and four soldiers and a trader. Indian etiquette having been satisfied, the Ottawas returned with their prizes to L'Arbre Croche. Not all ruffled feelings were soothed, however. A Chippewa chief who had been away during the attack was furious when he learned what had happened. He promptly killed the four prisoners to make up for his having missed the massacre.

The only British post left west of Detroit was the fort at Green Bay on the western side of Lake Michigan. Captain Etherington sent a message to the fort's commander, Lieutenant James Gorrell, describing the hopelessness of the situation and ordering him to abandon the fort and surrender to the Ottawas. Gorrell turned his fort over to a delegation of far western tribes, who wanted nothing to do with Pontiac's war, and took his garrison to L'Arbre Croche. There, the British officers managed to persuade the Ottawas to take their captives to Montreal and ransom them. The Chippewas objected, but the Ottawas departed on July 18 with their prisoners and reached Montreal, by way of the Ottawa River, less than a month later.

The War Moves East

All of the tribes of the western Great Lakes were now in the war on the side of Pontiac, and war belts were sent to the tribes to the east and south of Detroit. There was nothing that incited an Indian to war more than the news of another's success, and Pontiac's amazing string of victories must have made the prospect of war more attractive than ever before. The Delaware Indians, already excited by the preachings of their own prophet, took up the hatchet almost immediately and were soon joined by the Mingoes and the Shawnees. They attacked settlements in the vicinity of Fort Pitt, killing anyone — man, woman, or child — they found outside of a stockade.

Thus began the most brutal phase of Pontiac's war. The war in the west had been waged almost exclusively against British soldiers. The only civilians in the whole vast area were a few traders and the French *habit-*

ants. The traders were not spared, but the Indians carefully avoided harming the French. In the relatively thickly populated eastern frontier, however, almost all the settlers were British. Isolated settlements, small farms, and lone cabins dotted the area west of the Appalachian and Allegheny mountains — irresistible temptations to an Indian warrior in search of scalps and plunder. Throughout the war, this frontier was under continuous attack, and anyone unfortunate or foolish enough to travel alone or without heavy armed escort was soon missing. George Croghan, an influential trader and Indian agent, later estimated that more than 2,000 civilians were killed or captured during the war.

Captain Simeon Ecuyer, the commander at Fort Pitt, ordered all the settlers in the area into the fort, and prepared for a siege. Fort Pitt was the strongest fort west of Niagara. Ecuyer had 16 cannon and 250 men and felt confident he could handle any Indian attack. While Fort Pitt was besieged for more than a month, it was never seriously threatened. The same could not be said for the smaller forts that protected the trail from Fort Pitt to Lake Erie — Fort Venango (present-day Franklin, Pennsylvania), Fort Le Boeuf (Waterford, Pennsylvania), and Fort Presqu'Isle.

The Senecas, the most war-loving of the eastern tribes, entered the war as soon as they heard of the attack on Lieutenant Cuyler's detachment. They struck first at Fort Venango, where Lieutenant Francis Gordon commanded fifteen or sixteen men. On June 16 they gained entrance to the fort either by treachery or by force (since there were no survivors, the details are not known) and slaughtered the whole garrison. Lieutenant Gordon was taken alive and forced to write down the grievances the Senecas had against the English — the scarcity of powder and the number of forts the English were maintaining in their land. They then burned the fort and put Lieutenant Gordon to death.

The Senecas next moved north and struck at Fort Le Boeuf on June 18. Ensign George Price and his thirteen-man garrison managed to hold off the Indians until nightfall and then escape into the woods. Price and

[34]

his men made their way south to Venango, which they found destroyed, and then proceeded to Fort Pitt, where they arrived on June 26. Price had lost two men.

The Senecas' next objective was Presqu'Isle, a much stronger post containing twenty-nine men under the command of Ensign John Christie. The Senecas were joined by about two hundred warriors Pontiac had sent from Detroit to assist in taking the eastern forts. Among them was a renegade Englishman who had been adopted by a tribe and was now fighting with them. He knew something of scientific siege operations, for the Indians began digging entrenchments to protect themselves from the fire from the fort. From their concealed positions, they shot fire arrows into the fort. Christie and his men retired to the fort's blockhouse, where they could make a stronger stand. The blockhouse was set on fire, but the soldiers managed to put it out. The Indians began digging a protected trench to the fort, which the British could not prevent. The rest of the fort was burned, but the blockhouse managed to hold out the whole of the next day. By midnight the soldiers were exhausted, and Christie decided it was time to negotiate. He called out to the Indians, and the renegade Englishman answered him in his own language. He told Christie that the Indians only wanted to destroy the fort and that if the garrison surrendered they would be set free. Christie sent out two soldiers to talk terms with the Indians and incidentally to inspect their siegeworks. When the soldiers returned to report that the Indians' entrenchments were sound, Christie decided to surrender, provided that he and his command were allowed to return to Fort Pitt. The Indians agreed, but as soon as they occupied the fort they seized the soldiers and divided them among the various tribes.

The Ohio Indians continued to press their siege of Fort Pitt. On June 24, two Delaware Indians requested a council with Captain Ecuyer in which they informed him of the fall of the northern forts and advised him to surrender before the victorious tribes converged on Fort Pitt.

Ecuyer, whose garrison now numbered 338, felt more confident than ever that he could hold out. His only problem was that smallpox had broken out in the fort. Hoping to inflict the disease on the Indians, he gave the two Delawares a present of two blankets and a handkerchief from the smallpox hospital.

This first recorded instance of germ warfare has shocked modern commentators more than any other aspect of Pontiac's War. Indians had virtually no resistance to the white man's diseases, and Ecuyer's gift undoubtedly was the cause of a smallpox epidemic that hit the Delawares, the Mingoes, and the Shawnees shortly afterward. To Ecuyer, a Swiss mercenary, and to the majority of the people on the frontier, Indians were treacherous, unnaturally cruel savages who deserved to be exterminated by any means possible. General Amherst himself asked one of his commanders, "Could it not be contrived to send the smallpox among the disaffected tribes of Indians?" and at one time the general seriously considered importing English hunting dogs to bring the Indians to bay.

The British Strike Back

General Sir Jeffrey Amherst first learned of trouble with the Indians from dispatches sent by Ecuyer which reached him in New York on June 6, 1763. Ecuyer reported the attacks around Fort Pitt and rumors that Sandusky had fallen and Detroit was being attacked. Amherst, who was looking forward to his retirement, refused to believe that the trouble was serious. "I cannot entertain a thought that they [the Indians] have been able to cut off the garrison of the Detroit, or any of the posts where officers are stationed," he wrote to Sir William Johnson. Nevertheless, he began to take the necessary precautions. He alerted two companies of light infantry to march to Philadelphia and join Colonel Bouquet if a western expedition were needed.

When news of Lieutenant Cuyler's defeat reached Amherst, he sent his own aide, Captain James Dalyell, north to Niagara to prepare an expedition to Detroit, should one prove necessary. Dalyell was to collect reinforcements along the way. Amherst had nothing but contempt for Indians, and only grudgingly released his troops to put down their ceaseless and, to him, petty uprisings. When he received a dispatch from Gladwin on June 21, however, he was forced to admit that he had a full-scale insurrection on his hands. He ordered Dalyell to proceed to Detroit, and Bouquet to march to the relief of Fort Pitt.

The British sloop *Michigan*, which had sailed for Niagara at the time of Lieutenant Cuyler's defeat, now returned to Detroit with 54 men; again she was commanded by Cuyler. The sloop reached the Detroit River on June 21, 1763, and word of her approach was quickly carried on to Pontiac. It was probably with a feeling of relief that Pontiac assembled his warriors to intercept the ship. The longer the siege wore on, the more troublesome the various tribes assembled around Detroit became.

The Indians' traditions of warfare prevented them from making an all-out assault on the fort. It was unthinkable for an Indian to sacrifice his own life so that his fellow warriors could gain entrance to a fort. Surprise and sudden slaughter was his idea of warfare, and if there were the remotest possibility that he would be killed or wounded, he would have no part in it. The siege of Detroit, therefore, had been a passive one, without even the digging of entrenchments to keep the hordes of warriors occupied. (Pontiac, moreover, could find no one to advise him on the proper method of conducting a siege — that is, digging parallel trenches, throwing up breastworks, tunneling, etc.) The problem of supplies had aggravated old feuds. Whenever captured bateaux or pack trains contained quantities of rum, there promptly followed a drinking bout in which, inevitably, prisoners were killed.

[37]

Throughout the siege of Detroit, Major Gladwin remained imperturbable and refused to discuss terms with Pontiac until his two captured officers were returned to him. Meanwhile, he received various chiefs of the tribes encamped at Detroit, many of whom were beginning to repent of their actions. They all told Gladwin that they had been forced into the war by Pontiac; and two tribes, the Potawatomies and Hurons, had even sued for peace. Gladwin told them all to give up the war and return to their hunting before they were ruined. These defections took place even as each day brought fresh news of victories outside of Detroit. Considering the Indian characteristics of individuality and unpredictability, it was a miracle that Pontiac had kept his diverse group of warriors together as long as he had.

Pontiac's warriors lay in ambush on Turkey Island (present-day Fighting Island) as the *Michigan* started up the river on the evening of June 23. The wind died just as the sloop was opposite the island, and Captain Newman was forced to drop anchor. The delighted Indians waited until nightfall, and then silently set out in their canoes for the seemingly helpless vessel. Captain Newman, however, expected an attack, and had kept the 54 soldiers belowdecks, out of sight of the Indians. When a lookout spotted the approaching Indians, Newman ordered the soldiers on deck. When the Indians were within range, he gave the order to fire, and 54 muskets and the ship's cannon delivered a point-blank broadside. Fourteen Indians were killed and another 14 wounded, an astonishing loss when one considers that they had taken seven British forts with the loss of hardly a man. The surviving Indians raced to shore and made no more attempts to capture the ship. The *Michigan* did not have enough wind to make it to Detroit until June 30. As it passed a village of the Indians, Captain Newman fired a broadside of grapeshot into it, just for good measure, wounding several Indians. The *Michigan* then sailed victoriously to the fort and unloaded her reinforcements and 150 barrels of supplies and ammunition. Pontiac, seemingly secure in the middle of the North American continent, had felt the lethal sting of British sea power.

The peace treaty between England and France officially ending the French and Indian War was signed in London on February 20, 1763, but Gladwin did not learn of it until June. On July 2 he sent Lieutenant Cuyler outside the fort with a copy of the treaty to be read to the French *habitants*. The *habitants* were under increased pressure from Pontiac to join actively in his war on his side. Although they had no great love for the British, they knew it would be suicidal for them to side with Pontiac. Nevertheless, many of the younger men accepted Pontiac's war belt and became, in effect, outlaws. Pontiac had sent a party of these Frenchmen with the warriors who had attacked Forts Miamis and Ouiatenon. He instructed them to continue into the Illinois country and to inform the French commandant at Fort de Chartres, on the Mississippi, that he was waging war against the English and would need his aid. It was Pontiac's constant dream that a French army was on its way to help him expel the British "carrion dogs" from his country.

Earlier in the day on July 2, Lieutenant McDougall managed to escape from the Ottawa camp. He had tried to persuade Captain Campbell to come with him, but Campbell, who was rather fat and nearsighted, felt that he would lessen McDougall's chances to escape and chose to remain. On July 4 Gladwin sent a party of soldiers to attack and destroy an entrenchment that the Indians and their new French allies had constructed on some high ground north of the fort. After a short, sharp engagement, the Indians were driven off. Two of the Indians were killed, and a British soldier, who had lived among the Indians as a captive, scalped one of them in full view of the retreating warriors. Unfortunately, the Indian he scalped was a nephew of a powerful Chippewa chief. When the chief heard what had happened he stalked into Pontiac's camp and demanded that Captain Campbell be turned over to him. Pontiac complied, and the chief killed Campbell immediately. The body was thrown into the river to float downstream by the fort, where it was recovered by the British.

The other Ottawas were furious at the Chippewa chief's highhandedness, and they demanded a prisoner of the Hurons to kill in revenge. (Why a prisoner of the Hurons instead of the Chippewas is not clear.) The Hurons still held Ensign Pauli, the same commander of Sandusky who had been adopted by a widowed squaw. When he heard of the argument, Pauli decided to make his break. He outran his pursuers, swam the river, and was rescued by a party of soldiers who were returning from the sally against the entrenchment that had started the whole chain of events. Pauli, painted and half naked, with his hair shorn down to a scalp lock, reported to Gladwin and told him of Campbell's horrible death.

Two days later, Gladwin sent the *Michigan* up the river to shell Pontiac's camp. Ensign Pauli went along to help direct the fire. Although it did little damage, the shelling forced Pontiac to move his camp further away from the fort and the river. It also frightened the Potawatomies and the Hurons into defecting. They offered to Gladwin to bring in all their prisoners if the English agreed not to punish them for this war which, after all, was Pontiac's doing. Gladwin promised that he would put in a good word for them with General Amherst and that they should tell all the other tribes of his generous treatment of them. The Hurons turned over Lieutenant Christie, the commander at Presqu'Isle, and eight other captives.

It was clear to Pontiac that the sloop and the schooner were Gladwin's prime weapon and chief means of reinforcement, so he set out to eliminate them. He, or more likely one of his French allies, devised a plan to destroy the ships by the use of fire rafts. Four of the captured bateaux were tied together and filled with wood, bark, and other inflammable materials. On the night of July 9, the Indians set them afire and launched them into the river to drift down with the current and crash into the two ships. The crews saw the burning rafts coming from some distance away and easily avoided them by slipping one of their anchors and drifting out of the way. Pontiac modified his scheme. He had two rafts constructed, one of which was to be launched in the previous manner, the second to be launched so that it would drift into the ships after they had

[40]

The Indian fire rafts on the Detroit River. In this illustration, the fire rafts are erroneously depicted as war canoes. Actually, they were bateaux — clumsy, flat-bottomed boats. (New York Public Library)

slipped their anchors. On the night of July 11, the first raft was ignited and launched to drift down on the *Michigan.* The sloop fired a single cannon at the raft. The Indians holding the second raft became so frightened at this that they let it go before they had ignited it, and it drifted harmlessly away.

Pontiac's personal direction of the siege and his attempts to destroy Gladwin's ships revealed that he was far from being a military genius. Unfortunately for the British, neither was the man who set out to save Detroit.

The Battle of Bloody Bridge

Captain James Dalyell was a storybook British officer. Young and dashing, the second son of a baronet with the right connections, he had risen rapidly in a number of fashionable regiments. Assigned to America, he was soon made aide-de-camp to Amherst himself. The prospect of lifting the siege of Detroit and putting down the Indian uprising would have appealed to any ambitious and brave officer, but to Dalyell it must have been irresistible. By the time he reached Niagara, he had collected 220 men, among them Major Robert Rogers and 21 New York Provincials, many of whom might have served with the Rangers. Dalyell picked up 40 more men from the units stationed at Niagara and, putting his entire force of 260 men into 22 bateaux, set off across Lake Erie. He had been so eager to get going that he left without waiting for any armed escort ship, thus jeopardizing his whole command.

By the time Dalyell's flotilla reached the mouth of the Detroit River a heavy fog had rolled in. Without the cover of this fog, his whole force would probably have been forced back or shot to pieces while running the gauntlet of Indian villages that lined both sides of the river. Only one village spotted the bateaux, and then only in time for a short musket exchange in which fourteen of Dalyell's men were wounded. Hearing the firing, the garrison at Detroit lined the walls of the stockade, and Gladwin sent a party of volunteers out to investigate. Slowly the bateaux began to emerge from the fog, one by one, each crowded to the gunwales with red-coated British soldiers. The men on the stockade burst into cheers. It must have seemed to them that their long ordeal had at last ended.

Dalyell wasted no time in proceeding to smash the Indians. His relief of Detroit probably did not strike him as the miracle it was, and his contempt for Indians, which he had learned from Amherst, merely increased. He immediately proposed a surprise attack on the Indian camps. Gladwin pointed out to him that surprise was impossible, and that the Indians still outnumbered the reinforced garrison. Dalyell was unimpressed. General Amherst — and he must have emphasized that name slightly — had sent him not only to relieve Detroit, but to disperse the Indians. Although Gladwin was the young man's superior officer, he yielded to this argument and consented to the attack. There *was* a small chance of success, and if Dalyell's luck held, he might be able to bring it off.

Dalyell, whose right to lead the attack had never been questioned, assembled 247 officers and men, mostly from the reinforcements he had brought with him. Among these was Major Rogers, the ranking officer, who apparently was unperturbed that he was not in command. Before dawn on the morning of July 31 the men began moving out of the fort as quietly as possible. Attempts at concealment of their movements were futile. Pontiac had already been informed by his spies that the British were moving against him.

Dalyell's plan of attack was simple — or perhaps simple-minded. His men were simply to march north to Pontiac's camp, five miles from the fort, and there defeat him. The marching order consisted of an advance guard of 25 men commanded by Lieutenant Archibald Brown, the main body commanded by Dalyell and Captain Robert Gray, and a rear guard commanded by Captain James Grant. Two bateaux which had been converted into gunboats sailed beside the soldiers as they marched up the river road. Their purpose was to bring back dead and wounded and to cover the withdrawal. There was no inland flanking party.

It was still dark when the advance guard approached the narrow wooden bridge that crossed Parent's Creek, about two miles from the fort. When the first men reached the middle of the bridge a flashing wall of musket fire sprang up in an arc around them, followed by the deafening sound of the discharge of hundreds of weapons. Lieutenant Brown fell wounded on the bridge with half his platoon. The night was filled with the screams of the wounded, the war whoops of the Indians, the shouts of command. Soldiers from the center of the column charged the bridge and cleared the Indians from a ridge on the other side. Flanking fire tore into the column, and then, far to the rear, heavy firing came from the left. The rear guard was under attack! Dalyell received a wound

The ambush at Bloody Bridge. (New York Public Library)

in the thigh, but it must have meant nothing to him as he realized that he had marched into a deadly trap.

Pontiac had more than 400 warriors dispersed to meet the British. He had posted about 160 in a semicircle beyond the bridge and among the fences and houses of a *habitant*'s farm. His main body of 250 men he had sent inland to cut back to a position less than a mile above the fort. There they had lain quietly as they watched the British march north. Pontiac was finally showing his prowess as a war chief. He was not planning merely to turn the British back; he was planning to utterly destroy them.

[44]

Dalyell sent word back to Grant to keep the road open at all costs. The center of the column was heavily engaged. Major Rogers had found cover with a party of his men in a house beside the road and, using it as a blockhouse, covered the main body's flank. Rogers, the only British officer of the French and Indian War who had bested the Indians in every engagement he had fought with them, was now fighting for his life.

Dalyell, after conferring with Grant, who had occupied the houses and fences on the west side of the road and had managed to hold the Indians off, ordered a retreat. The withdrawal was an orderly one. One of the gunboats was sent back to the fort with a load of wounded, and the main body began withdrawing behind Rogers' covering fire. A party of Indians was entrenched in the excavation for a new house that lay not far from the road and their fire held up the retreat. The only way they could be routed was by a charge, and Dalyell led it. He was killed almost at once and Captain Gray took command and succeeded in driving the Indians from their cover. Captain Gray also was wounded, and was placed on one of the gunboats for the return to the fort. This left Captain Grant in command, since Major Rogers was still holding out in his blockhouse. The main force had retreated past him, and Rogers was now exposed to Indian fire on all sides.

When Grant heard of Rogers' predicament, he sent one of the gunboats upstream opposite the blockhouse to cover Rogers' retreat. He also sent Ensign Pauli with a detachment of 20 men to assist Rogers. (In the course of a few weeks Pauli had surely had one of the most adventurous careers in the British army.) Both tactics worked, and Rogers and his men escaped their dangerous position. The retreating column remained intact, with one section falling back under the protection of the one to the rear, until it had regained the fort. The time was eight o'clock in the morning. Casualties from the engagement were Dalyell and 19 men killed, three officers and 39 men wounded, three of whom later died. It is believed the Indians lost seven killed and twelve wounded. The bodies of the men who had fallen at the bridge stained the water red with blood, and thereafter Parent's Creek was known as Bloody Run, and the bridge as Bloody Bridge.

The victory at Bloody Bridge increased Pontiac's standing among his fellow Indians, but it did not really improve his position. The British had fought their way out of his trap and Fort Detroit was now stronger than ever. The two ships came and went at will, bringing in supplies and reinforcements and attacking the Indian villages with grapeshot and cannonballs. Gladwin, far from retiring within his fort while waiting for enough reinforcements to punish the Indians, maintained the offensive and continued to send out sorties to harass the Indians. Detroit was a stalemate, and any further victories would have to be sought elsewhere.

The Battle of Bushy Run

In the east, Colonel Bouquet was having trouble mounting his expedition for the relief of Fort Pitt. Travel over the wilderness roads was always difficult, but almost impossible with the huge supply wagons needed to sustain a marching army. Thousands of settlers were fleeing the frontier, and the panic-stricken civilians refused to act as wagoners for Bouquet. General Amherst had requested Pennsylvania's governor, James Hamilton, to assist the forces that would be moving through his colony. The Pennsylvania Assembly met on July 4 and with reluctance voted to provide wagons and to raise 700 men. They insisted, however, that they were not to take part in any offensive against the Indians.

Bouquet assembled his forces at Carlisle, Pennsylvania. He had a total of 460 men, including 214 from a Scottish regiment, the 42nd, known as the Black Watch. The army left Carlisle on July 18 and arrived at Fort Ligonier, 40 miles from Fort Pitt, on August 2. During the difficult march, Bouquet was informed of the fall of Venango and Presqu'Isle, two forts which he himself had established. He was also irritated by the refusal of the settlers in the areas through which he passed to render any assistance or even to take steps to defend themselves. He was obliged to leave companies of men along the way to garrison abandoned forts. A

Colonel Henry Bouquet, a Swiss mercenary and one of the ablest commanders in the British army. (Library of Congress)

complete military man, Bouquet's opinion of civilians was never very high, but he considered the Pennsylvanians downright cowardly. "I feel myself utterly abandoned," he wrote to Amherst, "by the very people I am ordered to protect."

By the time he reached Ligonier, Bouquet had not heard from Fort Pitt for more than a month. Assuming the worst, he decided to make a dash for the fort. (Actually, Fort Pitt had never been in real danger, and Ecuyer was in control of the situation. Furthermore, most of the Indians had been drawn off by the approach of Bouquet, whom they were hurrying to intercept in anticipation of a Braddock-like massacre.) Leaving behind the heavy wagons, Bouquet and his men hurried forward with the horses (350 of them) loaded only with flour.

[47]

On August 5, just twenty-six miles from Fort Pitt, Bouquet's advance guard was attacked. Two companies from the main force rushed up to assist and were soon heavily engaged all along the line. Bouquet ordered his main force to advance. The Highlanders were armed with inaccurate "Brown Bess" muskets, but their chief weapon was the bayonet. The men formed into a line and began moving through the forest underbrush. The remote hills of western Pennsylvania, echoing the beat of drums and the shrill shouts of officers, provided the backdrop for one of the most splendid and fearsome sights in the world — a general charge by a British regiment. The momentum of the charge cleared the area in front of the advance guard as the screaming Indians melted away into the forest. While the British were regrouping, both flanks received heavy fire. Firing from the rear indicated that the Indians were attempting to encircle them. Bouquet ordered his men to fall back on the supply horses. They formed a circle around the horses, whose terrified handlers were holding them at the top of a low hill. The sacks of flour they carried were used to form a circular barricade, inside of which were put the seriously wounded.

The fighting presently settled down to a series of skirmishes, with groups of Indians rushing forward to be dispersed by a bayonet charge from within the circle. It was hot work, and the British were without water on the hill. The Indians were confident and became more careful as the plight of the soldiers worsened. By nightfall, the situation seemed so desperate to Bouquet that he wrote a dispatch to General Amherst in which he expressed doubt that his army would last another day. "Whatever our fate may be," he wrote, "I thought it necessary to give your Excellency this early information . . . as, in case of another engagement, I fear insurmountable difficulties in protecting and transporting our provisions, being already so much weakened by the losses of this day, in men and horses, besides the additional necessity of carrying the wounded, whose situation is truly deplorable." Each man on the hill knew what his fate would be if captured, particularly the wounded, who even now were suffering agonies of thirst. The Indians continued to harass the troops throughout the night, making sleep impossible.

In the morning the Indians — Delawares, Mingoes, Shawnees, and Hurons from Sandusky — set up a general commotion, screaming their fierce cries and shouting insults and abuse in English. The firing became heavier, and the attacks against the circle increased in intensity and effectiveness. The long march, the full day of fighting, and the sleepless night had exhausted the soldiers. And the maddening thirst had driven many of them to the edge of despair. As the day wore on, the hill became a scene of complete horror. Many horses had been hit by musket fire and lay thrashing and kicking on the ground; others had broken loose and galloped, terrified, up and down the lines, causing further alarm and confusion. But the troops never broke, and Bouquet knew that as long as he had a body of disciplined men he could act. By now he knew every inch of his terrain, and he conceived a bold plan — the feigned retreat.

Two companies abandoned their posts as if to withdraw into the center of the circle. The companies on either side of them sent a thin line of men into the gap to cover their retreat, thus flattening the circle. The Indians, seeing this and sensing a panic among the British, pressed forward. Many warriors were drawn from other parts of the circle by this sudden chance to break through and wreak havoc among the confused troops. The thin line of troops on the flattened edge of the circle seemed about to give way, when a crashing volley from the side ripped into the closely grouped mass of attacking Indians. With hoarse cries from their parched throats, the fierce Highlanders of the Black Watch burst out of the forest in a headlong bayonet charge. They were the two companies of men who had retired into the middle of the circle, only to break out on the other side where a depression in the ground and covering trees shielded them from the Indians. They had quick-marched through the forest and come up on the flank of the excited and heedless Indians. At last they had the elusive foe where they wanted him, at the point of their bayonets.

[49]

The charge of the Black Watch was the first time in the long history of conflict between the white man and the Indian that the two sides had closed on a field of battle in a European-style engagement. The Indians turned to meet the charge, but soon broke and ran. Meanwhile, two more companies had sallied out of the circle on the other side and lay in wait for the retreating Indians. The Indians passed directly across their front. The Highlanders rose from their position, poured a volley into the fleeing Indians, and took up the charge. The rout was complete. The soldiers pursued the Indians through the forest as far as their strength would carry them. The British then regrouped and marched to the nearest water, which was at Bushy Run, about a mile away, and it was from this place that the battle took its name. Bouquet had lost fifty men killed, including three officers, sixty wounded, and five missing. The Indians had lost about the same, a crushing blow for a people who considered the loss of even one warrior a disaster. More important, among the Indian dead were two powerful Delaware chiefs, which may have discouraged that nation from further pursuing the war.

Bouquet's army proceeded to Fort Pitt, where they arrived on August 10. The wagons were brought up from Fort Ligonier, and then returned, carrying the beleaguered women and children to safety. The Indian threat in western Pennsylvania was over, and the siege of Fort Pitt was lifted.

The Massacre at Devil's Hole

In September, the Seneca Indians of western New York, who had taken little part in the war after their victories at Venango, Le Boeuf, and Presqu'Isle, began to take an interest in the portage route between Fort Niagara and Lake Erie. This was the most strategic spot on the continent, but it was also the most vulnerable. Supplies from the eastern seaboard and Canada were gathered at Fort Niagara, on the mouth of the Niagara River, and then loaded on boats which proceeded upriver to the foot of the escarpment through which the famous falls has cut

The Niagara River gorge, with Niagara Falls in the upper right-hand corner. The old portage road left the course of the river at Devil's Hole (located just beyond the hydroelectric power plant) and continued overland to Fort Schlosser, which was located at the end of the straight highway that cuts through the center of the photo. (Courtesy, Power Authority of the State of New York)

the Niagara gorge. Here they were unloaded and carried up to the top of the escarpment and along a road beside the gorge to a place where the river had formed a cave in the side of the gorge (called Devil's Hole), and then overland to Fort Schlosser, a small fort which stood well above the falls. There the supplies were loaded on boats and taken up through the rapids to the mouth of Buffalo Creek, where they were transferred to the ships from Detroit. There was hardly a spot on the entire trail that could not be successfully attacked from ambush.

On September 14, between three hundred and five hundred Seneca Indians lay in wait beside the trail that led close by Devil's Hole. Twenty-five wagons were returning down the trail from Fort Schlosser after having delivered their supplies. They were escorted by an officer and thirty soldiers. As they passed the part of the trail closest to the precipice, the Indians fired a volley into the whole convoy and then burst from their concealment and rushed onto the road. Horses reared and stampeded, some plunging over the edge and into the gorge below, carrying their drivers with them. The soldiers tried to rally, but were overwhelmed and in the hand-to-hand fighting that followed were either tomahawked or thrown over the cliff. Only two men managed to escape into the forest.

Two companies of soldiers, about eighty men, had been posted to guard the landing spot at the foot of the escarpment. Hearing the volley of the ambush, they hastily caught up their weapons and advanced up the trail on the run. The Indians were waiting for them at a new ambush point they had prepared about a mile below Devil's Hole. They caught the hurrying troops in close formation and their first volley felled about half of them. The Indians leaped onto the trail in overwhelming numbers and closed with the soldiers before they could fire a volley. Those who could, fled into the forest and made their way back to Niagara as the Indians fell to scalping and stripping the bodies.

The relief column sent out from Fort Niagara found a scene of complete carnage. The naked and scalped bodies of soldiers and teamsters lay strewn both on the trail and at the bottom of the gorge. Five officers and 67 men had been killed and eight wounded. The loss was greater than

Devil's Hole. The outline of the cave can be seen just to the right of the underpass. (Courtesy, Power Authority of the State of New York)

in any of the battles at Bloody Bridge, Bushy Run, or any of the forts. It is doubtful that the Indians lost a man!

The Siege of Detroit Is Lifted

On October 3, the schooner *Huron* arrived at Detroit with the disheartening news that the *Michigan* had been lost. Both ships had sailed from Detroit bearing wounded from the battle at Bloody Bridge. The

[53]

Michigan had started her return voyage on August 26, loaded with supplies and seventeen soldiers. She was caught in the middle of Lake Erie by a storm and was driven aground on the southeast shore. The crew and her passengers constructed a temporary fort and, after being reinforced from Niagara, beat off an attack by a band of Indians. The sloop was beyond repair, so when the *Huron* returned from Detroit, the *Michigan* was dismantled, her provisions, crew, and passengers loaded on the schooner, and all returned to Niagara.

The desultory action around Detroit was broken on September 2, when the *Huron* dropped anchor at the mouth of the Detroit River. It was delivering six Mohawk chiefs, sent by Sir William Johnson to dissuade the separate tribes from continuing the war. Some French spies learned that the commander, Captain Horsey, had only 22 men aboard as crew and guard. Pontiac was pleased at the prospect of giving his warriors some action, and he called for an attack on the ship that night. About 340 Ottawas and Chippewas (the Hurons were used to stall the six Mohawk chiefs) set off in their canoes as soon as it was dark. They got to within 100 yards of the schooner before they were discovered. The crew rushed to their battle stations as the Indians let out a savage roar and sped toward the boat. The *Huron* got off one blast from its bow gun before the Indians paddled under the bow and began climbing up the sides of the ship. The crew fought them off with swivel guns, muskets, pistols, and, finally, spears. Captain Horsey and a soldier were killed in the melee, and four of the crew were wounded.

A party of Indians had been hacking away at the *Huron*'s anchor cable and, when it suddenly parted, the ship swung around in the current and scattered the attacking canoes. This gave the six crewmen who were still able to fight the chance to use their swivel guns again. The mate, a man named Jacobs, shouted to his shipmates to fight to the death and directed that the last man alive set fire to the powder and blow up the ship. A white captive who had been fighting with the Indians heard this and warned the Indians of the danger of the ship's exploding. The In-

The attack on the schooner Huron *on the Detroit River. (New York Public Library)*

dians, who had probably had enough anyway, quickly broke off the engagement. They lost eight killed and 20 wounded; seven of the wounded later died. Again, this was a serious blow to the Indians. Pontiac was beginning to learn, as the nations of Europe had learned, that to fight the British on the water was a risky business.

On September 9, a group of Potawatomies from Fort St. Joseph came to Detroit and made peace with Gladwin. And for the first time a peace faction made itself heard among the Ottawas. When a group of Miamis came to Detroit to learn how the war was going, they found a divided camp. Half of the Miamis returned to the Maumee at once, the other waited to see what the other tribes would do. A prominent Mississaugi-Chippewa chief named Wabbicomigot held conferences with Gladwin inside the fort. Like all the Indians who had gone to Gladwin, he complained that he had been tricked by Pontiac into taking part in this

[55]

mistaken war, and that now he wished only forgiveness and peace. Furthermore, he interceded with Gladwin on behalf of all the chiefs who were disposed to make peace.

As a result, the Chippewas gave up six prisoners on October 14, the same day that the first snow fell. This reminder of the harsh winter ahead, a winter in which they and their families could perish if they did not start their hunting soon, prompted the chiefs of the other tribes to do the same. On October 17, the peace faction from the Ottawa camp sued for peace. The French *habitants* also made subtle moves to put them on better terms with the British. They began smuggling wheat into the fort, and the renegades among them started slipping away to the Illinois country.

Only Pontiac continued to pursue the siege. On October 29 there were four inches of snow. The same night a French officer arrived from Fort de Chartres bearing letters to Pontiac, the *habitants*, and Gladwin. Major de Villiers, the commander at De Chartres, had received official notification of the peace treaty between France and England, and now wished all the nations of the Great Lakes to "bury the hatchet" and live in peace and harmony with the British, their brothers. There would be no French army marching to the aid of Pontiac.

Pontiac's Capitulation

His dream crushed, Pontiac had no choice but to capitulate. He dictated a note that was translated into French by one of the *habitants* and delivered to Gladwin inside the fort. "My Brother," Pontiac said, "the word which my father has sent me to make peace I have accepted; all my young men have buried their hatchets. I think you will forget the bad things which have taken place for some time past. Likewise I shall forget what you may have done to me, in order to think of nothing but good. I, the Chippewas, the Hurons, we are ready to go speak with you when you ask us. Give us an answer. I am sending this resolution to you in order that you may see it. If you are as kind as I, you will make me a reply. I wish you a good day. [Signed] Pontiac."

Gladwin replied that since he had not started the war he could not end it as simply as that; however, he would inform General Amherst of Pontiac's message and inform him of the general's reply. Pontiac was never allowed inside the fort to consult with Gladwin. Gladwin did this for Pontiac's own safety; he felt that he could not control his men and the British traders if they ever got within reach of this man who had previously caused such mayhem and misery.

Gladwin, as much as he was gladdened by this sudden lifting of the siege, was saddened that the reinforcements he had expected for so long would now be useless for punishing the Indians. De Villiers, in his message, had offered sanctuary to any of the tribes who wished to retire west of the Mississippi. This meant that if the English sent a punitive force against the Indians, they would migrate west under French protection, thus destroying the English fur trade.

Nevertheless, Amherst had gathered enough men to reinforce his outposts and free their garrisons to join an expeditionary force to punish Pontiac and his warriors. Under the command of Major John Wilkins, 600 men set out from Niagara for Detroit on October 20 and were promptly attacked on the portage road. Two officers and six men were killed. The expedition proceeded to Lake Erie by way of Fort Schlosser, and embarked in boats for the voyage to Detroit. On the night of November 7, the flotilla was caught in one of the sudden, violent storms for which Lake Erie is notorious. They were driven to Pointe aux Pins (near Blenheim, Ontario), where they counted their losses of three officers and 67 men drowned, 18 boats with 52 barrels of supplies sunk, and two boats and their occupants missing. The inland sea, which had served the British so well, had finally exacted its fearful toll. Wilkins, after surveying his battered force, decided to return to Niagara.

Accordingly, Gladwin was once again left in isolation. Even though he was now receiving provisions from the *habitants*, the fort was too heavily garrisoned. Since there was no possibility of further action until the spring, he sent Major Rogers and two other officers with 240 men back to Niagara on bateaux. Gladwin must have felt some bitterness as he watched them depart. Although he had been promoted to the rank of lieutenant-colonel, the privations of the siege, the futility of his attacks against an enemy that melted away before him, and the failure to punish the Indians who had started this cruel war had finally cracked this steadfast commander. In October he had written to Sir William Johnson, "I am brought into a scrape and left in it; things are expected of me that can't be performed; I could wish I had quitted the service seven years ago, and that somebody else commanded here."

Gladwin's uncharacteristic complaining was nothing compared to Amherst's. As Pontiac's war had progressed, and one disaster followed another, his irritation with the Indians had turned to a pathological hatred. He instructed his commanders to take no prisoners, to execute any Indian who fell into their hands, to spread the pox among them, to eliminate this foul race by any means possible. His instructions, if followed to the letter, would have amounted to a program of genocide (racial extermination). In October he received the long-awaited permission to return to England. So, Amherst embarked on November 17, mercifully unaware of the disaster that had befallen Wilkins' expedition. Back in England, Sir Jeffery found that his splendid victories in the French and Indian War were forgotten; in fact, he became known as the general who could not put down an Indian uprising.

As for Pontiac, he had set off for the Illinois country with a handful of faithful followers to learn firsthand from the French why they would not join in driving the British from the land. He was going into virtual exile, since few of his village would have anything to do with him. He had practically ruined them. They had lost many warriors and had gained nothing. In the spring, after their winter hunting, their powder would be gone and their firearms in need of repair. If the English decided to punish them, they would be helpless. They were glad to see him go.

Thus, Pontiac's War was over. The captains and the chiefs, embittered and dissatisfied, had all departed, and Detroit lay under the deep winter snow.

Peacemaking

In reality, Pontiac had not sued for peace, but merely a truce. In the spring and summer of 1764 he was active among the Indians of the Illinois, who were still hostile toward the British. Pontiac continued to spread the lie that a great French army was on its way to help him drive the British from the land. Despite all his work, however, the tribes continued to defect. The Senecas had made peace with Sir William Johnson in the east, and even the British-hating Hurons at Sandusky had gone to Detroit and begged Gladwin for peace. The Ottawas themselves were split into two parties — a war party and a peace party — each maintaining a separate village on the Maumee River. The siege of Detroit was not resumed, mainly because of the lack of gunpowder. At a council with Sir William Johnson at Niagara, the Great Lakes Indians had pleaded with him to send traders among them again. Pontiac had indeed ruined them, as Gladwin had predicted, for they could not or would not give up the trade goods they had come to depend on.

General Amherst was succeeded by Major General Thomas Gage, to whom fell the task of finally punishing the rebellious Indians. Having inherited the forces that Amherst had built during the previous fall, he launched a two-pronged expedition into the Indian territory. Colonel Bouquet was to march from Fort Pitt through the Ohio country to destroy the villages of the Delaware and the Shawnee. Another army of 1,200 men, under the command of Colonel John Bradstreet, set sail from

Niagara. Its mission was to attack the Delawares and Shawnees in passing and to relieve the garrison at Detroit and establish a new garrison at Michilimackinac.

Unfortunately, Colonel Bradstreet was unfamiliar with Indian ways. He got no further than Presqu'Isle when a delegation of Shawnees and Delawares met him and asked for peace. Instead of sending them on to Johnson, who was the only person who had the authority to conclude a formal peace treaty, Bradstreet signed a treaty with them on August 12. He then sent a dispatch to Bouquet informing him that he need not punish these two nations. After securing a promise from the Indians to meet him at Sandusky and deliver their white prisoners to him, he sailed blithely on his way. While all this was taking place, Shawnee and Delaware war parties were again attacking the frontier. One party fell on an isolated schoolhouse and killed the defenseless teacher and all the nine pupils but one.

Bradstreet, intrigued with his role of peacemaker, decided to send an officer overland to Fort de Chartres to inform the French and the Indians of his treaty with the Delawares and Shawnees and to warn them against opposing the British troops who were on the way to occupy the French forts. The officer selected was Captain Thomas Morris. With an escort of Iroquois Indians and two French guides, he was set ashore at the mouth of the Maumee River.

At the very first Indian village he reached, Morris was confronted by Pontiac himself. Pontiac, hating the British, told Morris that a great French army was marching to his aid, and showed Morris a letter, "full of the most improbable falsehoods," to prove it. The next day Morris addressed a council of the neighboring chiefs, telling them of the peace treaty Bradstreet had made with the eastern tribes. This, combined with the testimony of the Iroquois that they had made peace with Sir William Johnson, impressed them so much that they sent two of their number to Detroit to make peace with Bradstreet.

None of these things pleased Pontiac, but he nevertheless allowed

Morris to proceed with his mission, and even offered him protection in the form of a belt of wampum — a sort of safe-conduct document. At the next village, Morris was met with hostility and was put under guard. A party of Delawares and Shawnees had preceded him to the village, spreading the tale of how they had duped Bradstreet and calling for a new uprising against the British. Morris, realizing that Bradstreet had been tricked, saw that his mission was futile. With the help of Pontiac's belt of wampum, he was able to obtain his release and made his way directly to Detroit.

Bradstreet had already reached Detroit and relieved Gladwin of his command. The indomitable defender of Detroit left his post with scarcely a look backward. On August 31 he boarded a ship for the east, never to return to the scene of his stubborn triumph. His father had died while Gladwin was besieged, and he had been named executor of the estate. He stopped at New York only long enough to arrange his retirement with General Gage, and left immediately afterwards for England. In the years to come, he was to marry and lead the calm and orderly life of a country gentleman in his native Derbyshire. He died in 1791.

Bradstreet, after relieving Gladwin, sent a detachment to Michilimackinac to reestablish the garrison there. He then turned again to peacemaking, for which he seems to have had great passion but little talent. He assembled all of the tribes around Detroit to a council at which all the Indian chiefs (only one of whom had been active in the war) asked to be forgiven all the bad things they had done under the spell of Pontiac. Bradstreet signed a peace treaty with them and obtained their promise that they would turn in their prisoners and acknowledge themselves subjects of the king of England, a concept meaningless to Indians. Bradstreet had intended also to demand the surrender of Pontiac, but decided not to mention him at the council, since Pontiac and his followers were living on the Maumee and were no longer allied with the Detroit Ottawas. He simply was not available for delivery. Anyway, Bradstreet was satisfied that he had brought peace to the area. His satisfaction was short lived, however, for news reached him shortly afterward that the Shawnees and Delawares were attacking the frontier. Bradstreet realized he had been tricked, and Captain Morris confirmed it when he rejoined the expedition.

Colonel Bouquet did not launch his expedition from Fort Pitt until October 1. With a force of 1,500 men, including Pennsylvania militia, he marched into the heart of the Delaware country. He wasted no time with the emissaries the Indians sent to plead against the destruction of their villages. He demanded the release of all their prisoners, and held hostages while their chiefs were sent to Sir William Johnson to plead for peace. Such a display of power impressed the tribes, and they capitulated one by one.

Bouquet proceeded as far as the forks of the Muskingum River and then marched back to Fort Pitt. With him came more than two hundred freed British prisoners, some of whom had by now spent much of their lives with the Indians and had been adopted into the tribes. Many of the younger captives remembered no other life, and often tried to escape the British and return to their Indian foster parents. The British were firm in their demands that all prisoners be released, for it was a serious point of honor with them. They found it difficult to accept that many of the captives preferred the ways of the Indian to those of civilization. So there was much sorrow that fall as Indian emissaries traveled from village to village collecting the captives who had become, in reality, members of their families.

Bouquet sent a Delaware and a Shawnee to the Illinois country to tell the tribes that they had submitted to the British. He wanted to counteract the first Delaware-Shawnee messengers who had urged a renewal of the war. In this way he hoped to dash any hopes Pontiac might have of recruiting more warriors for a new attack on the British. The mission was successful in persuading the Indians along the Maumee and the Wabash that the Ohio Indians had abandoned Pontiac.

The campaign season of 1764 ended with relative peace through-

Colonel Bouquet negotiating with the Indians on the Muskingum River, October 1764. From a drawing by Benjamin West. (New York Public Library)

out the Indian world. But the Indians who took part in the war had not been punished, and Pontiac was still at large. The British so far had not remotely threatened him.

Croghan's Mission

George Croghan, the Indian agent, was one of the few white men who could match the Indian in cunning. He had spent most of his life among Indians, both as trader and agent. He understood the Indian — indeed, at times, even thought like him — but he was thoroughly loyal to the Crown. The Indian was to be sympathized with, flattered, rewarded, or cheated, all to one end — to increase His Majesty's commerce in the New World. Croghan was the man assigned by Sir William Johnson to bring Pontiac to the treaty council and formally end this troublesome war.

Croghan was held up at Fort Pitt by the necessity of procuring a balanced delegation of Indians to accompany him. An advance party left on March 22, while Croghan conducted a congress with the Ohio Indians, who were bringing in the last of their prisoners. Croghan was unable to leave Fort Pitt until May 15. In the meantime, the advance party had reached Fort de Chartres and had actually met and negotiated with Pontiac, who had been drawn there to learn if the French peace with the English included the Illinois territory. Apparently Pontiac had finally been convinced that the Ohio Indians had indeed made peace with the British. This, combined with the French commander's confirmation of the terms of the peace treaty, must have disposed him toward making peace. Indeed, if Croghan had not been delayed, a treaty might have been concluded then and there. As it was, Indian vacillation, rumors spread by the French, and continued hostile acts by some of the tribes served to keep the situation unresolved. Several times the lives of the British were threatened by some fresh rumor or event that turned the assembled Indians against them.

Croghan's delay was justified, since his party was attacked by Kickapoo and Mascouten Indians on the Ohio River. Casualties were two white men and three Indians killed, and most of the rest of the party wounded, including Croghan. The party contained emissaries from the Delaware, Shawnee, and Seneca nations. The attacking Indians, who had been told by Frenchmen that the emissaries were Cherokees, their traditional enemies to the south, had made a dreadful mistake. They so feared retaliation from the Ohio and eastern tribes that they readily agreed to make peace with the British and allow them to repossess their forts. Pontiac's only remaining allies were thus taken away from him.

Croghan continued westward. Pontiac, more disposed to peace than ever, started eastward to meet him with delegates from the Illinois nations. The two parties met on the river and returned to Fort Ouiatenon for a formal council. Pontiac had finally been brought to the treaty table with an official representative of the British government.

During this council Pontiac insisted that one condition be included in the treaty: Namely, that since the French had only occupied their forts as tenants, the English victory did not entitle them to the land. In other words, the status of the white man had not changed; he resided in Indian territory only with the permission of the Indian. To Croghan, of course, this offer was ridiculous. He and his superiors considered the Indian territory a prize of war which was now their possession under international law (a body of rules agreed upon by the civilized nations of the world — that is, Europe). Croghan, however, agreed to Pontiac's demand, knowing full well that his superiors would never allow it to become part of a formal treaty.

Accordingly, the two parties then proceeded to Detroit, where on August 17 they were met by representatives of all the northern tribes, who had gathered in response to an invitation given by Bradstreet the year before. Pontiac entered the fort for the first time since his last meeting with Gladwin on May 8, 1763, not as the victorious leader of a war party, but as an unsuccessful war chief suing for peace. All of the chiefs took up Pontiac's argument that the French were merely tenants on the land and that they had paid for their right to occupy the forts with presents to the Indians. Again, Croghan went along with them. The only real result these demands had was that some settlers and traders around the forts purchased deeds from the Indians in order to strengthen their claims to the land. Pontiac himself signed several of these deeds.

Croghan, after securing a promise from the Indians to meet with Johnson in the spring, left for Niagara on September 26. The tribes dispersed to do their winter hunting. Fort de Chartres was occupied by the British on October 9, 1765. The terms of the treaty between France and England had finally been carried out.

The Death of Pontiac

On July 23, 1766, Pontiac and several western chiefs and Iroquois chiefs met with Johnson at Fort Ontario at Oswego, New York. The council lasted seven days, with Pontiac speaking for the western Indians. The negotiations merely formalized the agreements reached with Croghan the previous year. The Indians professed their desire to live in peace, promised to bring in any prisoners who had not yet been returned, and agreed to recall all war belts. Johnson promised to send more traders and gunsmiths to the forts and to reward the Indians with presents and powder.

Throughout the conference, Johnson deferred to Pontiac, addressing him directly, and generally behaving as though Pontiac were indeed the grand chief of the western tribes. Whether or not he did this intentionally, it did not please the other chiefs. There were rumors among them that Pontiac, in return for ending the war, was to receive a pension from the Crown. Pontiac, for his part, rose to the occasion, and in many of his speeches spoke as if for himself rather than for the other tribes. Presents were distributed to the Indians, and the council ended with both sides well pleased with themselves. Except for jealousy of Pontiac created by Johnson, the council had been a success.

Thus, Pontiac returned to his village on the Maumee River an ardent admirer of the British. Apparently he fulfilled all the promises he had made at Oswego. The Indian world was again in turmoil. Now that hostilities had ceased, settlers were again pouring over the mountains to settle the Ohio Valley. Technically this settlement was illegal, since no settlers were allowed west of the forks of the Ohio, but the small garrison at Fort Pitt was helpless to prevent it. Many war belts were passed among the Ohio and Illinois Indians, but Pontiac refused to accept any of them. This was an exact reversal of his position of 1763. Moreover, there was now a war faction among the Ottawas that broke away from Pontiac's peace faction, further reducing his small number of faithful followers. So, by 1768, Pontiac was in virtual exile, and the once-great warrior's activity was confined almost entirely to the peaceful pursuits of hunting and trading.

On April 20, 1769, Pontiac was in Cahokia, a French settlement on the eastern side of the Mississippi River across from the French fort of St. Louis. In the years since the council at Oswego he had been drawn increasingly to the Mississippi to trade. Somehow he had managed to antagonize the Indian tribes in the area. One of these tribes, the Peoria, feared retaliation by Pontiac for some unknown incident that had taken place the previous year. Assuming that Pontiac was still as powerful as he had been in the past, the Peorias interpreted his latest trip to Cahokia as a war party bent on revenge. Therefore, they decided to remove the imagined threat by assassinating him. Pontiac was unarmed as he left the trading post at Cahokia and stepped into the street. A Peoria brave who had accompanied him out of the store suddenly struck him from behind with his war club. Pontiac fell to the ground and the Peoria leaped on him and stabbed him. The great chief died almost immediately.

The Significance of Pontiac's War

In the entire history of human warfare, the place of Pontiac's War is not an important one. The battles, so momentous to the people involved, were mere skirmishes in the worldwide struggle among the nations of Europe. To the men whose task it was to put down the uprising and punish the guilty, it was something to be ended by any means and as soon as possible.

Yet to the settlers of the areas west of the Appalachian Mountains, it was the one single event which shaped their attitudes in the years to come. Pontiac's War convinced them of three things.

First, that "the only good Indian was a dead Indian." There literally was not a single family on the frontier that had not lost at least one of its members to the Indians. And the manner in which the Indians conducted their campaigns — the treachery, the indiscriminate killing of children as well as men and women, and the horrible tortures they inflicted on their captives — instilled in almost every person on the frontier a consuming hatred that was to be the dominant feature of all future relations between them and the Indians they dispossessed. This hatred was to make no distinction between Indian nations, whether peaceful or warlike, friendly or hostile.

Second, Pontiac's War convinced the settlers they could not depend on the army to protect them or to punish the Indians. The official view of the army was that the frontier people had no right to cross the mountains, and they were thus beyond their concern. During the French and Indian War, the settlers had been passive, leaving the fighting to the army. During Pontiac's War, however, they were roused by their hatred to strike back. Groups of settlers willingly formed expeditions to punish Indians in their area. Although these expeditions were rarely successful — and often punished the wrong Indians — they were numerous enough to become familiar to all able-bodied men and boys on the frontier. Thus was formed the frontier people's fierce self-reliance and a feeling of independence of their fellow citizens who lived calmly and safely in the towns of the seaboard. Furthermore, taxes were levied to support the armies that had fought, for the most part, so ineffectually. The people on the frontier were the first to deride and then to refuse to submit to taxation by the mother country.

Third, Pontiac's War brought home to the settlers of the frontier that they were indeed a people, a special breed whose destiny it was to tame the new land and subdue the Indains. It convinced them that they could not depend on the British government or their fellow colonists to support them or even help them to defend themselves. As a result, the settlers who pushed the frontier westward took with them a hatred for all Indians, a contempt for authority, and disdain for their fellow county-men in the East.

For the American Indians themselves, Pontiac's War was the beginning of the end. Their failure to achieve a clear-cut victory taught them nothing. Instead of seeking unity and confederation as the only effective opposition to the white man, each tribe made its separate peace and pursued its own ends. Instead of conciliating the white man on whom he had come to depend so much, the Indian openly expressed his contempt for him and continued to attack him when the occasion offered itself.

These fixed attitudes of the frontier people and the Indian were to run their parallel courses throughout the next century. They were to tarnish the white man's eventual triumph, and they were to hasten the destiny of the American Indian which was first glimpsed during Pontiac's War.

Selected Bibliography

Henry, Alexander. *Travels and Adventures in Canada and the Indian Territories Between 1760 and 1776.* Revised edition, New York, 1901.

Navarre, Robert. *Journal of the Conspiracy of Pontiac, 1763.* Translated by R. Clyde Ford. Detroit, 1910.

Parkman, Francis. *Conspiracy of Pontiac.* 2 vols. Boston, 1907.

Peckham, Howard H. *Pontiac and the Indian Uprising.* Princeton, 1947.

Van Every, Dale. *Forth to the Wilderness: The First American Frontier, 1754-1774.* New York, 1961.

Index